ONE-POT
MEALS

Consultant Editor:
Valerie Ferguson

southwater

Contents

Introduction

Everyone loves the idea of one-pot cooking, which conjures up thoughts of warming comfort-food, easy preparation, minimal washing-up and wonderful pans bubbling to the brim with delicious, rich stews.

All true, but the art of one-pot cooking goes much further. In this book we return to some basic cookery methods: braising, stir-frying, poaching and boiling. They may sound rather mundane but, with imagination and the amazingly wide range of ingredients available now, these techniques take on a new lease of life, giving us some of the most exciting flavours we've ever encountered.

Browse through the chapter on main course soups and discover how easy they are to make and, with the addition of herbs, spices and unusual ingredients, how delicious and exciting they can be. Stews and pot-roasts are not necessarily heavy dishes: some are light and fresh, according to the season, and some are vegetarian. There are delicious recipes for pasta, grains, noodles, stir-fries and sautés to provide you with endless ideas.

The recipes will become firm favourites for quick lunches, informal evening meals or more sophisticated dinner parties.

Equipment

Our guide helps you to decide whether you have all you require in your kitchen for successful one-pot cooking.

Pans It is important to buy the best pans you can afford; they'll definitely last a lot longer. Thin, flimsy pans burn quickly and scorch the contents and it can be difficult to maintain a constant temperature in them.

For soups, stews and pot-roasts, always make sure the pan is big enough. Check in the recipe whether the dish will need to go in the oven to finish cooking; if so, a flameproof casserole may be more suitable.

Woks and frying pans also play a major role in one-pot cooking. Make sure you buy the right wok for your type of cooker: if you cook on electric rings, you'll need one with a flat base that rests on the heat source.

Roasting Tins Choose a roasting tin in which the ingredients will fit comfortably, without overcrowding. Don't forget to check that the tin will fit inside your oven!

Above: It is well worth investing in good-quality saucepans and roasting tins.

Clockwise from top left: slotted spoons, pestle and mortar, measuring jug, measuring spoons, chopping knife, paring knife, zester.

Chopping Boards

A good-quality, thick board will last for years. Remember to keep separate boards for raw and cooked meats and fish.

Knives

Two essential knives should be in every kitchen. A chopping knife has a heavy, wide blade and comes in a variety of sizes. Choose one with a blade that is about 18–20 cm/7–8 in long; this makes the knife easy to handle and will be ideal for chopping vegetables, meats and fresh herbs. A paring knife has a small blade and is ideal for trimming and peeling all kinds of vegetables and fruits.

Measuring Jugs & Spoons

Measure ingredients carefully when following a recipe. Good measuring jugs and spoons make this far easier.

Zester

A useful tool for cutting long, thin strips of citrus rind.

Pestle & Mortar

If you use fresh spices, a pestle and mortar are perfect for crushing small amounts.

Slotted Spoon

A simple utensil, essential for one-pot cooking. When you lift browned meat from a pan, it leaves the fat and juices, so you don't lose valuable flavours.

Techniques

Chopping an Onion

Whether chopping finely or roughly, the basic method is the same.

1 Cut off the stalk end of the onion and cut it in half through the root, leaving the root intact. Remove the skin and place the halved onion, cut-side down, on the board. Make lengthways vertical cuts into the onion, taking care not to cut right through to the root.

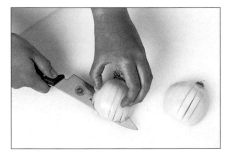

2 Make two or three horizontal cuts from the stalk end through to the root, but without cutting all the way through. Cut the onion across from the stalk end to the root. The onion will fall away in small squares. Cut further apart for larger squares.

Peeling Tomatoes

If you have the time, always peel tomatoes before adding them to sauces or stews.

1 Make a cross in each tomato with a sharp knife and place in a bowl. Pour over enough boiling water to cover and leave to stand for 30 seconds. The skins should start to come away. Slightly unripe tomatoes may take a little longer.

2 Drain the tomatoes and peel the skin away with a sharp knife. Don't leave the tomatoes in the boiling water for too long as they tend to soften.

Browning Meat

This is a very important process for adding flavour and colour when making stews and casseroles.

1 Heat a little oil in a pan until very hot. Add a few pieces of meat at a time, depending on the size of the pan, and allow it to turn a rich golden brown, turning to brown all sides. Don't add the meat all at once as this reduces the heat dramatically and the meat will stew instead of sealing.

2 Remove the meat from the pan with a slotted spoon, to drain off as much fat as possible, and place on kitchen paper. Repeat with the remaining meat.

Using a Wok

Many one-pot recipes are suitable for cooking in a wok.

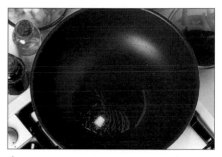

1 Have all the ingredients prepared and close to hand before you start. Heat the wok for a few minutes, then add the oil and swirl it around to coat the base and sides. Allow the oil to heat for a few moments, then use a small piece of onion to test to see whether the oil is sizzling hot.

2 Reduce the heat a little as you add the first ingredients. Stir-fry over quite a high heat, but not so high that food sticks and burns. Keep the ingredients moving with a long-handled spatula or wooden spoon. If a wok dish dries out, don't add any more ingredients as these may unbalance the intended flavour; simply add a splash of water.

Curried Salmon Chowder

The mild curry paste really enhances this soup.

Serves 4

INGREDIENTS

50 g/2 oz/4 tbsp butter
225 g/8 oz onions, coarsely chopped
10 ml/2 tsp mild curry paste
150 ml/¼ pint/⅔ cup white wine
300 ml/½ pint/1¼ cups
    double cream
50 g/2 oz creamed coconut, grated
350 g/12 oz potatoes, peeled and
    finely chopped
450 g/1 lb salmon fillet, skinned and cut
    into bite-size pieces
60 ml/4 tbsp chopped fresh
    flat leaf parsley
salt and freshly ground
    black pepper

1 Melt the butter in a large saucepan, add the onions and cook over a low heat for 3–4 minutes or until beginning to soften. Add the curry paste and cook for 1 minute more.

2 Add 475 ml/16 fl oz/2 cups water, the wine, cream, creamed coconut and a little seasoning. Bring to the boil, stirring until the coconut dissolves.

3 Add the potatoes and simmer, covered, for about 15 minutes or until almost tender. Gently stir in the fish, but do not break it up too much. Simmer very gently for 2–3 minutes or until just tender. Add the parsley, adjust the seasoning and serve.

Pasta & Lentil Soup

Serve this wholesome soup with crusty bread for a substantial supper.

Serves 4–6

INGREDIENTS
90 ml/6 tbsp olive oil
50 g/2 oz/⅓ cup ham or salt pork, cut into
   small dice
1 medium onion, finely chopped
1 celery stick, finely chopped
1 carrot, finely chopped
225 g/8 oz/1 cup dried green or brown
   lentils, soaked in water for 2–3 hours
2 litres/3½ pints/9 cups chicken stock or
   water, or a combination of both
1 fresh sage leaf or 1.5 ml/¼ tsp dried sage
1 fresh thyme sprig or 1.5 ml/¼ tsp
   dried thyme
175 g/6 oz/2 cups ditalini or other
   small soup pasta
salt and freshly ground black pepper

1 In a large saucepan, heat the oil and sauté the ham or salt pork for 2–3 minutes. Add the onion and cook gently until it softens.

2 Add the celery and carrot and cook for 5 minutes more, stirring frequently. Drain the lentils and stir into the vegetables in the pan.

3 Pour in the stock or water, add the herbs and bring to the boil. Cook over a moderate heat for about 1 hour or until the lentils are tender. Add salt and pepper to taste.

4 Stir in the pasta and cook it until it is just done. Allow the soup to stand for a few minutes before serving.

Squash, Bacon & Swiss Cheese Soup

A lightly spiced and substantial squash soup, enriched with smoked bacon and plenty of creamy, melting cheese.

Serves 4

INGREDIENTS

900 g/2 lb butternut squash
    or pumpkin
225 g/8 oz smoked back bacon
15 ml/1 tbsp oil
225 g/8 oz onions, coarsely chopped
2 garlic cloves, crushed
10 ml/2 tsp ground cumin
15 ml/1 tbsp ground coriander
275 g/10 oz potatoes, peeled and cut into
    small chunks
900 ml/1½ pints/3¾ cups
    vegetable stock
10 ml/2 tsp cornflour
30 ml/2 tbsp crème fraîche
Tabasco sauce, to taste
175 g/6 oz/1½ cups Gruyère
    cheese, grated
salt and freshly ground
    black pepper

1 Cut the butternut squash or pumpkin into large pieces. Using a sharp knife, carefully remove the skin from each piece, wasting as little of the flesh as possible.

2 Scoop out the seeds and chop the squash or pumpkin into small chunks. Remove all the fat from the bacon and roughly chop the meat.

3 Heat the oil in a large saucepan and cook the onions and garlic for 3 minutes or until they are beginning to soften.

4 Add the bacon and cook for about 3 minutes. Stir in the spices and cook for a further 1 minute.

5 Add the chopped squash or pumpkin to the pan with the potatoes and vegetable stock. Bring to the boil and simmer for 15 minutes or until the squash or pumpkin and potatoes are tender.

6 Blend the cornflour with 30 ml/ 2 tbsp water and add to the soup, with the crème fraîche. Bring to the boil and simmer, uncovered, for 3 minutes. Adjust the seasoning and add Tabasco sauce to taste. Ladle the soup into warmed bowls and sprinkle over the cheese; it will begin to melt. Serve the soup immediately.

Beef Noodle Soup

A steaming bowl, packed with delicious flavours and a hint of the Orient.

Serves 4

INGREDIENTS

10 g/¼ oz dried porcini mushrooms
6 spring onions
115 g/4 oz carrots
350 g/12 oz rump steak
about 30 ml/2 tbsp oil
1 garlic clove, crushed
2.5 cm/1 in piece fresh root ginger, peeled
    and finely chopped
1.2 litres/2 pints/5 cups beef stock
45 ml/3 tbsp light soy sauce
60 ml/4 tbsp dry sherry
75 g/3 oz thin egg noodles
75 g/3 oz spinach, shredded
salt and freshly ground black pepper

1 Break the mushrooms into small pieces, place in a bowl and pour over 150 ml/¼ pint/⅔ cup boiling water. Leave to soak for 15 minutes.

2 Shred the spring onions and carrots into fine strips, 5 cm/2 in long. Trim any fat off the steak and discard; slice the meat into thin strips.

3 Heat the oil in a large saucepan and cook the beef in batches until browned, adding a little more oil if necessary. Remove the cooked beef with a slotted spoon and drain on kitchen paper.

4 Add the garlic, ginger, spring onions and carrots to the pan and stir-fry briskly for 3 minutes.

5 Add the beef, beef stock, the mushrooms and their soaking liquid, the soy sauce, sherry and plenty of seasoning. Bring to the boil and simmer, covered, for 10 minutes.

6 Break up the noodles slightly and add to the pan, with the spinach. Simmer gently for 5 minutes or until the beef is tender. Adjust the seasoning and serve piping hot.

Vegetable & Herb Chowder

Potatoes, runner beans, celery, leek, onion and yellow or green pepper combine to make this thick, creamy soup a real meal-in-a-pot.

Serves 4

INGREDIENTS

1 onion
1 leek
1 celery stalk
1 yellow or green pepper
25 g/1 oz/2 tbsp butter
30 ml/2 tbsp chopped fresh parsley
15 ml/1 tbsp plain flour
1.2 litres/2 pints/5 cups
   vegetable stock
350 g/12 oz potatoes, peeled
   and diced
a few fresh thyme sprigs or 2.5 ml/½ tsp
   dried thyme
1 bay leaf
115 g/4 oz young runner beans, thinly sliced
   on the diagonal
120 ml/4 fl oz/½ cup milk
salt and freshly ground
   black pepper

1 Finely chop the onion, slice the leek and dice the celery. Seed and dice the yellow or green pepper.

COOK'S TIP: Remember to cut off the ends of the runner beans and remove the string from the sides. A bean slicer will make the slicing easier.

2 Melt the butter in a heavy-based saucepan or flameproof casserole and add the onion, leek, celery, yellow or green pepper and parsley. Cover and cook over a low heat until all of the vegetables are soft.

3 Add the flour and stir until well blended. Add the stock slowly, stirring to combine. Bring the mixture to the boil, stirring frequently.

4 Add the potatoes, fresh or dried thyme and the bay leaf. Simmer, uncovered, for about 10 minutes.

5 Add the sliced runner beans and continue to simmer the chowder for a further 10–15 minutes or until all the vegetables are tender.

6 Stir in the milk and season with salt and pepper. Heat through. Before serving, discard the thyme stalks and bay leaf. Serve hot in warmed bowls.

Fisherman's Stew

The fish is cooked quickly in a rich, herby tomato and smoked bacon sauce – even people who claim not to like fish will be converted.

Serves 4

INGREDIENTS
6 streaky bacon rashers, cut into strips
15 g/½ oz/1 tbsp butter
1 large onion, chopped
1 garlic clove, finely chopped
30 ml/2 tbsp chopped
   fresh parsley
5 ml/1 tsp fresh thyme leaves or
   2.5 ml/½ tsp dried thyme
450 g/1 lb tomatoes, peeled,
   seeded and chopped, or canned
   chopped tomatoes
150 ml/¼ pint/⅔ cup dry vermouth
   or white wine
450 ml/¾ pint/scant 2 cups
   fish stock
275 g/10 oz potatoes, diced
675–900 g/1½–2 lb skinless white fish
   fillets, cut into large chunks
salt and freshly ground black pepper
sprig of fresh parsley, to garnish

1 Fry the bacon in a large saucepan over a moderate heat until lightly browned but not crisp. Remove from the pan and drain on kitchen paper.

2 Add the butter to the pan and, when it has melted, add the onion. Cook, stirring occasionally, for 3–5 minutes or until soft.

3 Add the garlic and herbs and continue cooking for 1 minute. Add the tomatoes, vermouth or wine and stock and bring to the boil.

4 Reduce the heat, cover and simmer the stew for 15 minutes. Add the potatoes, cover again and simmer for a further 10–12 minutes or until they are almost tender.

5 Add the chunks of fish and the bacon. Simmer gently, uncovered, for 5 minutes or until the fish is just cooked and the potatoes are tender. Adjust the seasoning and serve, garnished with parsley.

COOK'S TIP: To make fish stock, simmer white fish heads, bones and trimmings with sliced onion, carrot, celery and lemon, a bay leaf, a few parsley sprigs, black peppercorns, water and a little white wine for 25 minutes. Strain, store in the fridge and use within two days or freeze for up to three months.

Mediterranean Fish Stew

This is delicious served with a rich garlic mayonnaise and plenty of crusty bread to mop up the juices. Use as many different varieties of fish and shellfish as you can find.

Serves 4

INGREDIENTS
450 g/1 lb mixed fish fillets,
    such as red mullet, monkfish, sea bass
    and/or mackerel
450 g/1 lb mixed uncooked shellfish,
    such as mussels and prawns
pinch of saffron strands
60 ml/4 tbsp olive oil
350 g/12 oz onions, coarsely chopped
350 g/12 oz fennel, halved and thinly sliced
    (about 1 small bulb)
10 ml/2 tsp plain flour
400 g/14 oz can chopped
    tomatoes, strained
3 garlic cloves, crushed
2 bay leaves
30 ml/2 tbsp chopped fresh thyme
pared rind of 1 orange
salt and cayenne pepper
garlic mayonnaise and crusty bread,
    to serve

1 Wash the fish, skin if necessary and cut into large chunks. Clean the shellfish and remove the heads from the prawns.

2 Place the saffron strands in a bowl and pour over 150 ml/¼ pint/⅔ cup boiling water. Leave the saffron to soak for about 20 minutes. Strain.

3 Heat the oil in a large saucepan and add the onions and fennel. Fry gently for 5 minutes, stirring occasionally, or until beginning to soften.

4 Stir in the flour. Gradually blend in 750 ml/1¼ pints/3 cups water, the tomatoes, garlic, bay leaves, thyme, orange rind, saffron liquid and seasoning to taste. Bring to the boil.

5 Reduce the heat, add the chunks of fish (not the shellfish) and simmer very gently, uncovered, for about 2 minutes.

6 Add the shellfish and cook for a further 2–3 minutes or until all the fish is cooked but still holding its shape. Discard any mussels that have not opened. Adjust the seasoning. Serve the stew in warmed bowls, topped with a generous spoonful of garlic mayonnaise and accompanied by plenty of crusty bread.

Chicken with Chianti

Together the robust, full-flavoured red wine and the red pesto give this sauce a rich colour and an almost spicy flavour, while the grapes add a delicious sweetness.

Serves 4

INGREDIENTS
45 ml/3 tbsp olive oil
4 part-boned chicken
    breasts, skinned
1 medium red onion
30 ml/2 tbsp red pesto
300 ml/½ pint/1¼ cups Chianti
300 ml/½ pint/1¼ cups water
115 g/4 oz red grapes, halved lengthways
    and seeded, if necessary
salt and freshly ground
    black pepper
fresh parsley,
    to garnish
rocket salad, to serve

1 Heat 30 ml/2 tbsp of the oil in a large frying pan, add the chicken breasts and sauté over a medium heat for about 5 minutes until they have changed colour on all sides. Remove with a slotted spoon and drain on kitchen paper.

> VARIATIONS: Use green pesto instead of red, and substitute a dry white wine such as Pinot Grigio for the Chianti, then finish with seedless green grapes. Add a few spoonfuls of mascarpone cheese at the end if you like, to enrich the sauce.

2 Cut the onion in half, through the root. Trim off the root, then slice the halves lengthways to make thin wedges.

3 Heat the remaining oil in the pan, add the onion wedges and red pesto and cook gently, stirring constantly, for about 3 minutes until the onion is softened, but not browned.

4 Add the Chianti and water to the pan and bring to the boil, stirring, then return the chicken to the pan and add salt and pepper to taste.

5 Reduce the heat, cover and simmer gently for 20 minutes or until the chicken is tender, stirring occasionally.

> COOK'S TIP: Use part-boned chicken breasts in preference to boneless chicken for a better flavour. Chicken thighs or drumsticks could also be cooked in this way.

6 Add the grapes to the pan and cook over a low to medium heat until heated through, then taste the sauce and adjust the seasoning as necessary. Serve hot, garnished with parsley and accompanied by the rocket salad.

Pot-roast Chicken with Lemon & Garlic

This is a rustic dish that is easy to prepare. Lardons are thick strips of bacon fat; if you can't get them, use streaky bacon.

Serves 4

INGREDIENTS
30 ml/2 tbsp olive oil
25 g/1 oz/2 tbsp butter
175 g/6 oz/1 cup smoked lardons or
   streaky bacon, coarsely chopped
8 garlic cloves
4 onions, quartered
10 ml/2 tsp plain flour
600 ml/1 pint/2½ cups
   chicken stock
2 lemons, thickly sliced
45 ml/3 tbsp chopped fresh thyme
1 oven-ready chicken,
   about 1.5 kg/3–3½ lb
2 x 400 g/14 oz cans flageolet beans,
   drained and rinsed
salt and freshly ground
   black pepper
bread, to serve

1 Preheat the oven to 190°C/375°F/ Gas 5. Heat the olive oil and butter in a flameproof casserole that is large enough to hold the chicken with a little extra room around the sides. Add the lardons or bacon and cook until golden, turning occasionally. Remove with a slotted spoon and drain on kitchen paper.

2 Brown the whole garlic cloves and the onions over a high heat until the edges are caramelized. Stir in the flour, then pour in the chicken stock. Return the cooked bacon to the pan with the sliced lemons, thyme and the salt and freshly ground black pepper.

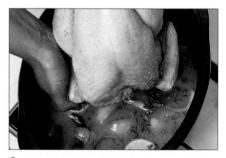

3 Bring the mixture to the boil, then place the chicken on top, season and transfer to the oven. Cook for 1 hour, basting the chicken occasionally with the cooking juices.

4 Baste the chicken once again with the juices. Stir the beans into the pan and return to the oven for a further 30 minutes or until the chicken is cooked through and tender.

5 Carve the chicken into thick slices and serve with the beans. Accompany with plenty of bread for mopping up.

Kashmiri Chicken Curry

A wonderful blend of spices with piquant apples makes this quickly cooked curry a special meal.

Serves 4

INGREDIENTS
10 ml/2 tsp corn oil
2 medium onions, diced
1 bay leaf
2 cloves
2.5 cm/1 in cinnamon stick
4 black peppercorns
1 small chicken, about 675 g/1½ lb, skinned
   and cut into 8 pieces
5 ml/1 tsp garam masala
5 ml/1 tsp crushed ginger
5 ml/1 tsp crushed garlic
5 ml/1 tsp salt
5 ml/1 tsp chilli powder
15 ml/1 tbsp ground almonds
150 ml/¼ pint/⅔ cup plain yogurt
2 green dessert apples, peeled, cored
   and sliced
15 ml/1 tbsp chopped fresh coriander
15 g/½ oz flaked almonds, lightly toasted,
   and fresh coriander leaves, to garnish

1 Heat the oil in a non-stick wok or frying pan and fry the onions with the bay leaf, cloves, cinnamon and peppercorns for about 3–5 minutes.

2 Add the chicken pieces and continue to stir-fry the mixture for at least 3 minutes until the chicken is no longer pink on the outside.

3 Lower the heat and add the garam masala, ginger, garlic, salt, chilli powder and ground almonds and continue to stir for 2–3 minutes.

4 Gradually pour in the plain yogurt and stir for a couple more minutes. Add the apples and chopped coriander. Cover and cook for about 10–15 minutes.

5 Check that the chicken is cooked through and serve immediately, garnished with the flaked almonds and whole coriander leaves.

Lamb Goulash with Tomatoes & Peppers

In this East European dish the meat and colourful vegetables are stewed slowly together on top of the stove until they are blissfully tender.

Serves 4–6

INGREDIENTS

30 ml/2 tbsp vegetable oil or
  melted lard
900 g/2 lb lean lamb, trimmed and cut
  into cubes
1 large onion, roughly chopped
2 garlic cloves, crushed
3 green peppers, seeded and diced
30 ml/2 tbsp paprika
2 x 400 g/14 oz cans chopped
  plum tomatoes
15 ml/1 tbsp chopped fresh
  flat leaf parsley
5 ml/1 tsp chopped fresh marjoram
30 ml/2 tbsp plain flour
salt and freshly ground black pepper
green salad, to serve

2 Add the onion and garlic and cook for a further 2 minutes before adding the green peppers and paprika.

3 Pour in the tomatoes and enough water, if needed, to cover the meat in the pan. Stir in the herbs. Bring to the boil, turn down the heat, cover and simmer very gently for 1½ hours or until the lamb is tender.

1 Heat the oil or lard in a frying pan. Fry the pieces of lamb for 5–8 minutes or until browned on all sides. Season well.

COOK'S TIP: Lamb is a tender meat and various cuts can be used for stewing in dishes such as this.

4 Blend the flour with 60 ml/4 tbsp cold water and pour into the stew. Bring back to the boil, then reduce the heat to a simmer and cook the stew until the sauce has thickened.

5 Taste the stew and adjust the seasoning as necessary. Serve with a crisp green salad.

Pot-roast Glazed Lamb

The vegetables in this pot-roast become caramelized, absorbing all the delicious flavours of the meat. Spoon the juices over during cooking.

Serves 6

INGREDIENTS
12 garlic cloves
1.2 kg/2½ lb leg of lamb (knuckle end)
about 12 small fresh rosemary sprigs,
    plus extra to garnish
45 ml/3 tbsp olive oil
12 shallots
900 g/2 lb potatoes, cut
    into chunks
675 g/1½ lb parsnips, cut into
    large chunks
675 g/1½ lb carrots, cut into chunks
300 ml/½ pint/1¼ cups red wine
45 ml/3 tbsp clear honey
30 ml/2 tbsp dark soy sauce
10 ml/2 tsp plain flour
475 ml/16 fl oz/2 cups lamb stock
salt and freshly ground
    black pepper

1 Preheat the oven to 190°C/375°F/ Gas 5. Peel and slice three of the garlic cloves. Make slits all over the meat and insert slices of garlic and small sprigs of rosemary. Season well.

2 Heat the oil in a large, flameproof casserole or roasting tin and add the whole shallots. Cook, stirring occasionally, until they begin to turn golden brown.

3 Add the potatoes, parsnips, carrots and remaining unpeeled garlic cloves. Stir to coat in the oil and season. Place the lamb on top and pour over half of the red wine. Cover tightly, place in the oven and cook for 1 hour, basting occasionally with any fat and juices.

4 In a small bowl, mix together the honey and soy sauce. After the first hour of cooking, pour the honey mixture over the lamb and baste. Return to the oven, uncovered, for a further 1–1¼ hours, basting the meat and vegetables from time to time.

5 Test that the meat is cooked and the vegetables are tender. Remove from the pan and leave the meat to rest for 10–15 minutes before carving (keep the vegetables warm).

6 Place the casserole or roasting tin on the hob, stir in the flour and cook for 1 minute. Blend in the stock and remaining wine, then bring to the boil and adjust the seasoning to taste. Serve the meat and vegetables with plenty of sauce spooned over them, garnished with sprigs of rosemary.

Veal Shanks with Tomatoes & White Wine

This famous Milanese dish is rich and hearty. As it is very filling, a mixed leaf salad is the ideal accompaniment.

Serves 4

INGREDIENTS
30 ml/2 tbsp plain flour
4 pieces veal shank
2 small onions
30 ml/2 tbsp olive oil
1 large celery stick, finely chopped
1 medium carrot, finely chopped
2 garlic cloves, finely chopped
400 g/14 oz can chopped tomatoes
300 ml/½ pint/1¼ cups dry
   white wine
300 ml/½ pint/1¼ cups chicken or
   veal stock
1 strip thinly pared lemon rind
2 bay leaves, plus extra to
   garnish (optional)
salt and freshly ground black pepper
mixed leaf salad, to serve

FOR THE GREMOLATA
30 ml/2 tbsp finely chopped fresh
   flat leaf parsley
finely grated rind of 1 lemon
1 garlic clove, finely chopped

1 Preheat the oven to 160°C/325°F/ Gas 3. Season the flour with salt and pepper and spread it out in a shallow bowl. Add the pieces of veal and turn them in the flour until evenly coated. Shake off any excess flour.

2 Slice one of the onions and separate it into rings. Heat the oil in a large, flameproof casserole, then add the veal, with the onion rings, and brown the meat on both sides over a medium heat. Remove the veal shanks with tongs and set aside on kitchen paper to drain.

3 Chop the remaining onion and add it to the pan with the celery, carrot and garlic. Stir the bottom of the pan to incorporate the pan juices and sediment. Cook gently, stirring frequently, for about 5 minutes until the vegetables soften slightly.

4 Add the chopped tomatoes, wine, stock, lemon rind and bay leaves, then season to taste with salt and pepper. Bring to the boil, stirring. Return the veal to the pan and coat with the sauce. Cover and cook in the oven for 2 hours or until the veal feels tender when pierced with a fork.

5 Meanwhile, to make the gremolata, mix together the parsley, lemon rind and garlic in a small bowl.

COOK'S TIP: Veal shanks are available from large supermarkets and good butchers. Choose pieces about 2 cm/¾ in thick.

6 Remove the casserole from the oven and lift out and discard the strip of lemon rind and the bay leaves. Taste the sauce and adjust the seasoning. Serve the stew hot, sprinkled with the gremolata and garnished with extra bay leaves, if you like, accompanied by a mixed leaf salad.

Polish Casserole

A marvellous combination of pork, venison, beef and garlicky sausage with vegetables and spices, this is Poland's national dish, known as *Bigos*.

Serves 8

INGREDIENTS
15 g/½ oz/¼ cup dried mushrooms
225 g/8 oz/1 cup stoned prunes
225 g/8 oz lean boneless pork
225 g/8 oz lean boneless venison
225 g/8 oz chuck steak
225 g/8 oz *kielbasa* (see Cook's Tip)
25 g/1 oz/¼ cup plain flour
45 ml/3 tbsp olive oil
2 onions, sliced
60 ml/4 tbsp dry Madeira
900 g/2 lb can or packet sauerkraut, rinsed
4 tomatoes, peeled and chopped
4 cloves
5 cm/2 in cinnamon stick
1 bay leaf
2.5 ml/½ tsp dill seeds
600 ml/1 pint/2½ cups stock
salt and freshly ground black pepper
chopped fresh parsley, to garnish
boiled new potatoes, tossed in chopped
    parsley, to serve (optional)

1 Soak the dried mushrooms and prunes in boiling water in a bowl. Leave for 30 minutes, then drain.

2 Cut the pork, venison, chuck steak and *kielbasa* sausage into 2.5 cm/1 in cubes and toss together in the flour. Heat the oil in a large, flameproof casserole and gently fry the onions for 10 minutes, then remove from the pan.

3 Add the meat to the pan in several batches and fry for about 5 minutes or until well browned; remove and set aside. Add the Madeira and simmer for 2–3 minutes, stirring.

4 Return the meat to the pan with the onions, sauerkraut, tomatoes, cloves, cinnamon, bay leaf, dill seeds, mushrooms and prunes. Pour in the stock and season with salt and pepper.

5 Bring to the boil, cover and simmer gently for 1¾–2 hours or until the meat is very tender. Uncover for the last 20 minutes to let the liquid evaporate, as the stew should be thick.

6 Sprinkle with chopped parsley. Serve immediately with boiled new potatoes, tossed in chopped parsley, if using.

COOK'S TIP: *Kielbasa* is a garlic-flavoured pork and beef sausage, but any similar type of continental sausage can be used. Use dried porcini mushrooms, if possible.

Cassoulet

Based on the traditional French dish, this recipe is full of delicious flavours and makes a welcoming and warming meal.

Serves 6

INGREDIENTS
450 g/1 lb boneless duck breast
225 g/8 oz thick-cut streaky pork or
   unsmoked streaky bacon rashers
450 g/1 lb Toulouse or garlic sausages
45 ml/3 tbsp oil
450 g/1 lb onions, chopped
2 garlic cloves, crushed
2 x 425 g/15 oz cans cannellini beans,
   rinsed and drained
225 g/8 oz carrots, coarsely chopped
400 g/14 oz can chopped tomatoes
15 ml/1 tbsp tomato purée
1 bouquet garni
30 ml/2 tbsp chopped fresh thyme
475 ml/16 fl oz/2 cups chicken stock
115 g/4 oz/2 cups fresh breadcrumbs
salt and freshly ground
   black pepper
fresh thyme sprigs, to garnish (optional)
salad leaves, to serve

1 Preheat the oven to 160°C/325°F/Gas 3. Cut the duck breast and pork or bacon rashers into large pieces. Twist the Toulouse or garlic sausages and cut into short lengths.

2 Heat the oil in a large, flameproof casserole. Cook the meat in batches, until well browned. Remove from the pan with a slotted spoon and drain on kitchen paper.

3 Add the onions and garlic to the pan and cook for 3–4 minutes or until beginning to soften, stirring frequently.

4 Stir in the beans, carrots, tomatoes, tomato purée, bouquet garni, thyme and seasoning. Return the meat to the pan and mix until well combined.

5 Add enough of the chicken stock just to cover the meat and cannellini beans. (The cassoulet shouldn't be swimming in juices, but if the mixture becomes too dry, add a little more stock or water.) Bring to the boil. Cover tightly and cook in the oven for 1 hour.

6 Remove the cassoulet from the oven, add a little more stock or water, if necessary, and discard the bouquet garni. Sprinkle over the breadcrumbs and return to the oven, uncovered, for a further 40 minutes or until the meat is tender and the top crisp and brown. Garnish with fresh thyme sprigs, if using, and serve with salad.

Root Vegetable Casserole

This hearty and sustaining dish is perfect for chilly winter days.

Serves 4–6

INGREDIENTS
15 ml/1 tbsp sunflower oil
knob of butter
15 ml/1 tbsp demerara sugar
450 g/1 lb unpeeled baby new potatoes
225 g/8 oz small onions
225 g/8 oz carrots, cut into large chunks
225 g/8 oz parsnips, cut into large chunks
400 ml/14 fl oz/1⅔ cups vegetable stock
15 ml/1 tbsp Worcestershire sauce
15 ml/1 tbsp tomato purée
5 ml/1 tsp wholegrain mustard
2 bay leaves
salt and freshly ground black pepper
chopped fresh parsley, to garnish

1 Heat the oil, butter and sugar in a pan. Stir until the sugar dissolves. Add the potatoes, onions, carrots and parsnips. Sauté for 10 minutes until the vegetables look glazed.

2 Mix the stock, Worcestershire sauce, tomato purée and mustard in a jug. Stir well, then pour over the vegetables. Add the bay leaves. Bring to the boil, then lower the heat, cover and cook gently for about 30 minutes until the vegetables are tender.

3 Remove the bay leaves. Add salt and pepper to taste and serve sprinkled with chopped parsley.

Chick-peas & Artichoke Bake

For a last-minute supper this is a quick, extremely tasty and unusual dish.

Serves 4

INGREDIENTS
400 g/14 oz can chick-peas, drained
    and rinsed
400 g/14 oz can black-eyed beans, drained
    and rinsed
130 g/4½ oz jar artichoke antipasti (or
    canned artichoke hearts, chopped, plus a
    little olive oil)
1 red pepper, seeded and chopped
1 garlic clove, crushed
15 ml/1 tbsp chopped fresh parsley
5 ml/1 tsp lemon juice
150 ml/¼ pint/⅔ cup soured cream
1 egg yolk
50 g/2 oz/½ cup grated cheese
salt and freshly ground black pepper

1 Preheat the oven to 180°C/350°F/
Gas 4. Mix the chick-peas, black-eyed
beans, artichoke antipasti or artichoke
hearts and chopped red pepper
together in a casserole.

2 Stir in as much of the artichoke
dressing, or oil if using artichoke
hearts, as is necessary to moisten the
mixture. Stir in the garlic, parsley,
lemon juice and salt and freshly
ground black pepper to taste.

3 Mix together the soured cream, egg
yolk, cheese and seasoning. Spoon
evenly over the vegetables and bake for
25–30 minutes or until the top is
golden brown. Serve hot.

Cheesy Courgette Casserole

A simple-to-prepare dish of sliced courgettes layered with Cheddar cheese and baked in an egg and milk custard.

Serves 4

INGREDIENTS
1 garlic clove, bruised
30 ml/2 tbsp olive oil or
   melted butter
1 kg/2¼ lb courgettes
225 g/8 oz/2 cups coarsely grated
   Cheddar cheese
2 eggs
350 ml/12 fl oz/1½ cups milk
salt and freshly ground
   black pepper
fresh parsley sprigs,
   to garnish

2 Cut the courgettes into 5 mm/¼ in slices. Place them in a bowl and toss with the remaining oil or melted butter. Add salt to taste.

1 Preheat the oven to 190°C/375°F/Gas 5. Rub the bruised garlic clove around the inside of an ovenproof dish, pressing hard against the dish to extract the juice; discard the garlic clove afterwards. Grease the dish lightly with a little of the olive oil or the melted butter.

3 Arrange half the courgette slices in an even layer in the prepared dish. Sprinkle with half the cheese. Add the remaining courgette slices, spreading them evenly on top.

VARIATION: For a spicier version, toss the courgettes with 5–10 ml/1–2 tsp chilli powder.

4 Place the eggs and milk in a jug with a little seasoning and whisk together. Pour over the courgettes. Sprinkle with the remaining cheese.

5 Cover with foil and bake for about 30 minutes, then bake uncovered for 30–40 minutes, until browned. Serve hot, warm, or cold, garnished with parsley.

Black Pasta with Raw Vegetables

Black pasta derives its dramatic colour from the addition of squid ink.

Serves 4

INGREDIENTS
3 garlic cloves, crushed
30 ml/2 tbsp white tarragon vinegar
5 ml/1 tsp Dijon mustard
90 ml/6 tbsp extra virgin olive oil
5 ml/1 tsp finely chopped fresh thyme
1 yellow pepper
1 red pepper
225 g/8 oz mangetouts
6 radishes
4 ripe plum tomatoes
1 avocado
275 g/10 oz black pasta
salt and freshly ground
    black pepper
6 fresh basil leaves, to garnish

1 In a bowl, blend together the garlic, vinegar, mustard, oil and thyme. Season to taste. Cut the peppers into diamond shapes, discarding the seeds. Halve the mangetouts and slice the radishes. Peel, seed and dice the tomatoes. Peel, stone and slice the avocado.

2 Place all the vegetables in a large bowl and add the dressing, stirring thoroughly to mix. Cook the pasta in plenty of boiling, slightly salted water according to the packet instructions until *al dente*. Drain and tip into a large, shallow, warmed serving dish. Cover with the vegetables and serve immediately, garnished with fresh basil leaves.

Sun-dried Tomato & Parmesan Carbonara

Double the ingredients to serve four. Serve with a crisp green salad.

Serves 2

INGREDIENTS
175 g/6 oz tagliatelle
50 g/2 oz sun-dried tomatoes in olive
    oil, drained
2 eggs, beaten
150 ml/¼ pint/⅔ cup double cream
15 ml/1 tbsp wholegrain mustard
50 g/2 oz/⅔ cup Parmesan cheese, grated
12 fresh basil leaves, shredded
salt and freshly ground black pepper
fresh basil leaves, to garnish
crusty or garlic bread, to serve

1 Cook the pasta in boiling, salted water according to the packet instructions until it is *al dente*.

2 Meanwhile, cut the sun-dried tomatoes into small pieces. In a bowl, beat together the eggs, cream and mustard with plenty of seasoning until well combined.

3 Drain the cooked pasta and immediately return it to the hot saucepan with the cream and egg mixture, sun-dried tomatoes, grated Parmesan cheese and shredded basil.

4 Return to a very low heat for 1 minute, stirring gently until the mixture thickens slightly. Adjust the seasoning and serve immediately, garnished with basil leaves. Serve with crusty or garlic bread.

Gingered Chicken Noodles

A blend of ginger, spices and coconut milk flavours this quick and delicious supper dish. For a real Oriental touch, add a little fish sauce just before serving.

Serves 4

INGREDIENTS

350 g/12 oz skinless, boneless
  chicken breasts
225 g/8 oz courgettes
275 g/10 oz aubergine
about 30 ml/2 tbsp oil
5 cm/2 in piece fresh root ginger, peeled
  and finely chopped
6 spring onions, sliced
10 ml/2 tsp Thai green curry paste
400 ml/14 fl oz/1⅔ cups coconut milk
475 ml/16 fl oz/2 cups chicken stock
115 g/4 oz medium egg noodles
45 ml/3 tbsp chopped fresh coriander,
  plus extra, to garnish
15 ml/1 tbsp lemon juice
salt and freshly ground black pepper

2 Heat the oil in a large saucepan and cook the chicken until golden. Remove with a slotted spoon and drain on kitchen paper.

3 Add a little more oil, if necessary, and cook the ginger and spring onions for 3 minutes. Add the courgettes and cook for 2–3 minutes or until beginning to turn golden. Stir in the curry paste and cook for 1 minute.

1 Cut the chicken breasts into bite-size pieces. Halve the courgettes lengthways and roughly chop them. Cut the aubergine into pieces about the same size as the courgettes.

VARIATION: Try substituting cooked peeled prawns for the chicken, adding them just a few minutes before serving.

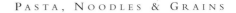

4 Add the coconut milk, stock, aubergine and chicken and simmer for 10 minutes. Add the noodles and cook for a further 5 minutes or until they are tender and the chicken is cooked.

5 Stir in the coriander and lemon juice and adjust the seasoning to taste. Serve garnished with extra coriander.

Paella

Based on the classic Spanish recipe, this dish combines a mixture of cooked seafood with aromatic saffron rice.

Serves 6

INGREDIENTS
about 30 ml/2 tbsp olive oil
2 red peppers, seeded and coarsely chopped
225 g/8 oz onions, coarsely chopped
2 garlic cloves, crushed
115 g/4 oz streaky bacon,
    coarsely chopped
350 g/12 oz/scant 1¾ cups long grain
    white rice
pinch of saffron strands
475 ml/16 fl oz/2 cups vegetable or
    chicken stock
300 ml/½ pint/1¼ cups dry white wine
350 g/12 oz ripe tomatoes
450 g/1 lb mixed cooked seafood,
    such as prawns, mussels and squid
115 g/4 oz/1 cup frozen peas, thawed
45 ml/3 tbsp chopped
    fresh parsley
salt and freshly ground black pepper
whole cooked prawns and mussels in
    their shells, to garnish

1 Heat the oil in a paella pan. Cook the peppers for 3 minutes or until beginning to soften; remove from the pan with a slotted spoon and drain on kitchen paper.

2 Add a little more oil to the pan and cook the onions, garlic and bacon for about 5 minutes, or until the onions have softened slightly, stirring.

3 Add the rice to the pan and cook for 1 minute until it begins to turn translucent. Stir in the saffron, vegetable or chicken stock, wine and seasoning. Boil, then simmer, covered, for 12–15 minutes, stirring occasionally.

4 Meanwhile, quarter the tomatoes and scoop out the seeds. Roughly chop the flesh.

VARIATION: You could make a vegetarian version of this dish by substituting one chopped aubergine and two chopped courgettes for the bacon and seafood.

5 When the rice is cooked and most of the liquid absorbed, add the tomatoes, seafood, peas and peppers. Heat gently, stirring occasionally, for about 5 minutes or until piping hot.

6 Stir in the parsley and adjust the seasoning before serving, garnished with the whole prawns and mussels.

Smoked Salmon Kedgeree

You could also try this recipe with grilled or poached fresh salmon.

Serves 6

INGREDIENTS

275 g/10 oz/scant 1½ cups long grain
    white rice
25 g/1 oz/2 tbsp butter
30 ml/2 tbsp olive oil
115 g/4 oz fine green beans, trimmed
1 onion, coarsely chopped
2 garlic cloves, crushed
1 red pepper, seeded and coarsely chopped
5 ml/1 tsp mild curry paste
115 g/4 oz cooked peeled prawns
175 g/6 oz smoked salmon or smoked
    salmon trimmings, coarsely chopped
grated rind and juice of 1 lemon
60 ml/4 tbsp mixed chopped fresh dill
    and chives
salt and freshly ground black pepper
lemon wedges and dill sprigs, to garnish
crusty bread, to serve

1 Cook the rice for about 12 minutes in boiling, salted water until just tender, but still retaining a little bite. Rinse in boiling water and drain well.

2 Rinse out the pan and heat the butter and oil. Halve the beans. Cook the onion, garlic, red pepper and beans for 5 minutes or until beginning to soften. Add the curry paste and cook for a further minute. Add the prawns and rice and stir over a low heat until both are piping hot.

3 Add the smoked salmon and grated lemon rind, plus lemon juice to taste. The salmon will begin to turn opaque. Adjust the seasoning and stir in the herbs. Serve immediately, garnished with lemon wedges and dill sprigs, accompanied by crusty bread.

Lamb Pilau

Both lamb fillet and minced lamb are used in this fruited rice dish.

Serves 4

INGREDIENTS
50 g/2 oz/scant ½ cup raisins
115 g/4 oz/½ cup stoned prunes
15 ml/1 tbsp lemon juice
25 g/1 oz/2 tbsp butter
1 large onion, chopped
450 g/1 lb lamb fillet, trimmed and
    cut into 1 cm/½ in cubes
225 g/8 oz/1¼ cups lean minced lamb
2 garlic cloves, crushed
600 ml/1 pint/2½ cups lamb stock
350 g/12 oz/scant 2 cups
    long grain rice
large pinch of saffron
salt and freshly ground
    black pepper
flat leaf parsley sprigs, to garnish

1 Cover the raisins and prunes with water. Add the lemon juice. Soak for 1 hour. Drain, then chop the prunes. Heat the butter in a pan and cook the onion for 3 minutes. Add the lamb, mince and garlic. Fry for 5 minutes, stirring, until the meat is browned.

2 Pour in 150 ml/¼ pint/⅔ cup of lamb stock and bring to the boil. Lower the heat, cover and simmer for 1 hour or until the lamb is tender. Add the remaining stock and bring to the boil.

3 Stir in the rice and saffron. Cover and simmer for 15 minutes or until the rice is tender. Stir in the raisins, prunes and seasoning. Serve hot, garnished with flat leaf parsley.

Couscous Aromatique

The cuisine of Morocco and Tunisia has many wonderful dishes using the wheat grain, couscous, which is steamed over simmering spicy stews. A little of the fiery harissa paste stirred in at the end adds an extra zing.

Serves 4–6

INGREDIENTS
450 g/1 lb/2⅔ cups couscous
60 ml/4 tbsp olive oil
1 onion, cut into chunks
2 carrots, cut into thick slices
4 baby turnips, halved
8 small new potatoes, halved
1 green pepper, seeded and cut
   into chunks
115 g/4 oz green beans, halved
1 small fennel bulb, sliced thickly
2.5 cm/1 in cube fresh root ginger,
   peeled and grated
2 garlic cloves, crushed
5 ml/1 tsp ground turmeric
15 ml/1 tbsp ground coriander
5 ml/1 tsp cumin seeds
5 ml/1 tsp ground cinnamon
45 ml/3 tbsp red lentils
400 g/14 oz can chopped tomatoes
1 litre/1¾ pints/4 cups stock
60 ml/4 tbsp raisins
rind and juice of 1 lemon
salt and freshly ground black pepper
ready-made harissa paste,
   to serve (optional)

1 Cover the couscous with cold water and soak for 10 minutes. Drain and spread out on a tray for 20 minutes, stirring it occasionally with your fingers.

2 Meanwhile, in a large saucepan, heat the oil and fry the vegetables for about 10 minutes, stirring from time to time.

3 Add the ginger, garlic and spices, stir well and cook for 2 minutes. Pour in the lentils, tomatoes, stock and raisins. Season with salt and pepper.

4 Bring to the boil, then turn down to a simmer. By this time the couscous should be ready for steaming. Place in a steamer and fit this on top of the stew.

5 Cover and steam gently for about 20 minutes. The grains should be swollen and soft. Fork through and season well. Spoon into a serving dish.

6 Add the lemon rind and juice to the stew and check the seasoning. If liked, add harissa paste to taste; it is quite hot, so beware! Spoon the couscous on to individual plates and ladle the stew on top.

Stir-fried Vegetables with Monkfish

A tastily spiced and quickly cooked one-pot fish meal.

Serves 4

INGREDIENTS
30 ml/2 tbsp corn oil
2 medium onions, sliced
5 ml/1 tsp crushed garlic
5 ml/1 tsp ground cumin
5 ml/1 tsp ground coriander
5 ml/1 tsp chilli powder
175 g/6 oz monkfish,
    cut into cubes
30 ml/2 tbsp fresh
    fenugreek leaves
2 tomatoes, seeded and sliced
1 courgette, sliced
15 ml/1 tbsp lime juice
salt

1 Heat the oil in a non-stick wok or frying pan and fry the onions over a low heat until soft.

2 Meanwhile mix together the garlic, cumin, coriander and chilli powder. Add this spice mixture to the onions and stir for about 1 minute.

3 Add the fish and continue to stir-fry for 3–5 minutes until the fish is well cooked through.

4 Add the fenugreek, tomatoes and courgette, followed by salt to taste, and stir-fry for a further 2 minutes. Sprinkle with lime juice before serving.

Thai Fish Stir-fry

This is best served with bread, for mopping up all the spicy juices.

Serves 4

INGREDIENTS

675 g/1½ lb mixed seafood (for example,
  red snapper, cod, raw prawn tails),
  filleted and skinned
300 ml/½ pint/1¼ cups coconut milk
15 ml/1 tbsp vegetable oil
salt and freshly ground black pepper
crusty bread, to serve

FOR THE SAUCE
5 cm/2 in piece fresh root ginger
2 large fresh red chillies
1 onion, coarsely chopped
5 cm/2 in piece lemon grass
5 cm/2 in piece galangal,
  peeled and sliced
6 blanched almonds, chopped
2.5 ml/½ tsp ground turmeric
2.5 ml/½ tsp salt

1 Cut the filleted fish into large chunks. Peel the prawns, keeping their tails intact.

2 To make the sauce, peel and slice the ginger and seed and chop the chillies. Discard the outer leaves of the lemon grass and roughly slice the inner leaves. Put all the ingredients in a food processor with 45 ml/3 tbsp of the coconut milk. Blend until smooth.

3 Heat a wok, then add the oil. When the oil is hot, add the prepared mixed seafood and stir-fry for 2–3 minutes. Remove from the wok.

4 Add the sauce and the remaining coconut milk to the wok, then return the seafood. Bring to the boil and season well with salt and freshly ground black pepper. Serve with crusty bread.

Stir-fried Crispy Duck

This stir-fry would be delicious wrapped in flour tortillas or steamed Chinese pancakes, with a little extra warm plum sauce.

Serves 2

INGREDIENTS

275–350 g/10–12 oz boneless duck breast
30 ml/2 tbsp plain flour
60 ml/4 tbsp oil
1 bunch spring onions, halved lengthways
   and cut into 5 cm/2 in strips
275 g/10 oz green cabbage,
   finely shredded
225 g/8 oz can water chestnuts, drained
   and sliced
50 g/2 oz/½ cup unsalted
   cashew nuts
115 g/4 oz cucumber, cut into strips
45 ml/3 tbsp plum sauce
15 ml/1 tbsp light soy sauce
salt and freshly ground black pepper
sliced spring onions, to garnish

2 Heat the oil in a wok or large frying pan and cook the duck over a high heat until golden and crisp. Keep stirring to prevent the duck from sticking. Remove with a slotted spoon and drain on kitchen paper. You may need to do this in batches.

3 Add the spring onions to the pan and cook for 2 minutes. Stir in the cabbage and cook for 5 minutes or until softened and golden.

1 Trim a little of the fat from the duck and thinly slice the meat. Season the flour well and use it to coat each piece of duck.

4 Return the duck to the pan with the sliced water chestnuts, cashews and the strips of cucumber. Stir-fry for 2 minutes.

5 Add the plum sauce and soy sauce with plenty of seasoning and heat for 2 minutes. Serve piping hot, garnished with sliced spring onions.

Sweet-&-sour Pork Stir-fry

This is a great idea for a quick family supper. Remember to cut the carrots into thin strips so that they cook in time.

Serves 4

INGREDIENTS
450 g/1 lb pork fillet
30 ml/2 tbsp plain flour
45 ml/3 tbsp oil
1 onion, coarsely chopped
1 garlic clove, crushed
1 green pepper, seeded
    and sliced
350 g/12 oz carrots, cut
    into strips
225 g/8 oz can bamboo
    shoots, drained
15 ml/1 tbsp white wine vinegar
15 ml/1 tbsp soft brown sugar
10 ml/2 tsp tomato purée
30 ml/2 tbsp light soy sauce
120 ml/4 fl oz/½ cup light vegetable stock
salt and freshly ground black pepper

2 Heat the oil in a wok or large frying pan and cook the pork over a medium heat for about 5 minutes until golden and cooked through. Remove with a slotted spoon and drain on kitchen paper. You may need to do this in batches.

3 Add the onion and garlic to the pan and cook for 3 minutes. Stir in the green pepper and carrots and stir-fry over a high heat for 6–8 minutes or until beginning to soften slightly.

1 Thinly slice the pork. Place the flour in a bowl and add seasoning. Toss the pork in the flour to coat.

4 Return the meat to the pan with the bamboo shoots. Add the remaining ingredients with the stock and bring to the boil. Simmer gently for 2–3 minutes or until piping hot. Adjust the seasoning, if necessary, and serve immediately.

Balti Lamb Sauté with Cauliflower

Cauliflower and lamb go beautifully together. This curry is given a final *tarka* of cumin seeds and curry leaves, which enhances the flavour.

Serves 4

INGREDIENTS
10 ml/2 tsp corn oil
2 medium onions, sliced
7.5 ml/1½ tsp grated fresh
    root ginger
5 ml/1 tsp chilli powder
5 ml/1 tsp crushed garlic
1.5 ml/¼ tsp ground turmeric
2.5 ml/½ tsp ground coriander
30 ml/2 tbsp fresh
    fenugreek leaves
275 g/10 oz boned lean spring lamb,
    cut into strips
1 small cauliflower, cut into
    small florets
300 ml/½ pint/1¼ cups water
30 ml/2 tbsp fresh coriander leaves
½ red pepper, seeded and sliced
15 ml/1 tbsp lemon juice

FOR THE TARKA
10 ml/2 tsp corn oil
2.5 ml/½ tsp white cumin seeds
4–6 curry leaves

1 Heat the oil in a wok or frying pan and fry the onions until golden brown. Lower the heat and add the ginger, chilli powder, garlic, turmeric and ground coriander, followed by the fresh fenugreek leaves.

2 Add the lamb strips to the wok and stir-fry until the meat is completely coated with the spices. Add half the cauliflower florets and stir well.

3 Pour in the water, cover the wok, lower the heat and allow to cook for 5–7 minutes until the cauliflower and lamb are almost cooked through.

4 Add the remaining cauliflower, half the fresh coriander, the red pepper and lemon juice and stir-fry for about 5 minutes, making sure that the sauce does not catch on the wok.

5 Check that the lamb is completely cooked, then transfer the contents of the wok to a warmed serving dish and keep warm.

COOK'S TIP: If you wish, you may use a good-quality olive oil for the *tarka* instead of the corn oil.

6 To make the tarka, heat the oil and fry the cumin seeds and curry leaves for about 30 seconds. While it is still hot, pour the seasoned oil over the cauliflower and lamb and serve garnished with the remaining fresh coriander leaves.

Vegetable Stir-fry with Eggs

A perfect family supper dish, this is very easy to prepare and is delicious served with crusty bread: Italian ciabatta is particularly good. Ask your butcher to cut the ham thickly in one piece.

Serves 4

INGREDIENTS

30 ml/2 tbsp olive oil
1 onion, coarsely chopped
2 garlic cloves, crushed
175 g/6 oz cooked ham
225 g/8 oz courgettes
1 red pepper, seeded and thinly sliced
1 yellow pepper, seeded and
    thinly sliced
10 ml/2 tsp paprika
400 g/14 oz can chopped tomatoes
15 ml/1 tbsp sun-dried tomato paste
    or tomato purée
4 eggs
115 g/4 oz/1 cup Cheddar cheese, grated
salt and freshly ground black pepper
crusty bread, to serve

1 Heat the oil in a deep frying pan and cook the onion and garlic for 4 minutes or until starting to soften.

2 Meanwhile, cut the ham and courgettes into batons or strips 5 cm/ 2 in long. Set the ham aside.

3 Add the courgettes and peppers to the onion and cook over a medium heat for 3–4 minutes or until beginning to soften.

4 Stir in the paprika, tomatoes, sun-dried tomato paste or purée, ham and seasoning. Bring to the boil and simmer gently for 15 minutes or until the vegetables are just tender.

5 Reduce the heat to low. Make four wells in the tomato mixture, break an egg into each and season. Cook over a gentle heat until the egg white just begins to set.

6 Preheat the grill to high. Sprinkle the cheese over the eggs and vegetables in the pan. Protect the handle with a double layer of foil, then place the frying pan under the grill for about 5 minutes until the cheese is golden and the eggs are lightly set. Serve at once with plenty of crusty bread.

Potato, Red Onion & Feta Frittata

This Italian omelette is cooked with vegetables and cheese, and is served flat, rather like a Spanish tortilla. Cut it into wedges and serve it, warm or cold, with a tomato salad.

Serves 2–4

INGREDIENTS
25 ml/1½ tbsp olive oil
1 red onion, sliced
350 g/12 oz cooked new potatoes, halved
  or quartered if large
6 eggs, lightly beaten
115 g/4 oz/1 cup feta
  cheese, diced
salt and freshly ground
  black pepper

3 Preheat the grill to high. Season the beaten eggs, then pour the mixture over the onion and potatoes. Sprinkle the cheese on top and cook over a moderate heat for 5–6 minutes until the eggs are just set and the base of the frittata is lightly golden.

1 Heat the oil in a large, heavy-based frying pan. Add the sliced red onion and sauté for 5 minutes until softened, stirring occasionally.

2 Add the cooked new potatoes and cook for a further 5 minutes until golden, stirring to prevent them sticking. Spread the mixture evenly over the base of the pan.

4 Place the pan under the grill (protect the pan handle with a double layer of foil if it is not flameproof) and cook the top of the frittata for about 3 minutes until set and lightly golden. Serve warm or cold, cut into wedges.

This edition is published by Southwater

Distributed in the UK by
The Manning Partnership,
251-253 London Road East, Batheaston,
Bath BA1 7RL, UK
tel. (0044) 01225 852 727
fax (0044) 01225 852 852

Distributed in Australia by
Sandstone Publishing,
Unit 1, 360 Norton Street, Leichhardt,
New South Wales 2040, Australia
tel. (0061) 2 9560 7888
fax (0061) 2 9560 7488

Distributed in New Zealand by
Five Mile Press NZ,
PO Box 33-1071, Takapuna,
Auckland 9, New Zealand
tel. (0064) 9 4444 144
fax (0064) 9 4444 518

Southwater is an imprint of Anness Publishing Limited

© 2000 Anness Publishing Limited

Publisher: Joanna Lorenz
Editor: Valerie Ferguson
Series Designer: Bobbie Colgate Stone
Designer: Andrew Heath
Editorial Reader: Marion Wilson
Production Controller: Joanna King

Recipes contributed by: Alex Barker,
Angela Boggiano, Carla Capalbo,
Catherine Clements, Roz Denny, Patrizia Diemling,
Sarah Edmonds, Nicola Graimes, Shehzad Husain,
Norma Macmillan, Maggie Pannell, Liz Trigg,
Laura Washburn, Elizabeth Wolf-Cohen,
Jeni Wright

Photography: William Adams-Lingwood,
Steve Baxter, Ian Garlick, Michelle Garrett,
Katharine Hawkins, Amanda Heywood,
Ferguson Hill, Janine Hosegood, Dave Jordan,
Michael Michaels, Thomas Odulate

Notes:
For all recipes, quantities are given in both metric
and imperial measures and, where appropriate,
measures are also given in standard cups
and spoons.
Follow one set, but not a mixture, because they
are not interchangeable.

Standard spoon and cup measures are level.

1 tsp = 5 ml   1 tbsp = 15 ml

1 cup = 250 ml/8 fl oz

Australian standard tablespoons are 20 ml.
Australian readers should use 3 tsp in place of
1 tbsp for measuring small quantities of gelatine,
cornflour, salt, etc.

Medium eggs are used unless otherwise stated.

1 3 5 7 9 10 8 6 4 2